K A Z U K I B U I S H I

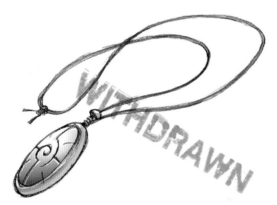

BOOK ONE
THE STONEKEEPER

AN IMPRINT OF
■SCHOLASTIC

ISBN 978-0-439-84680-6 (hardcover)
ISBN 978-0-439-84681-3 (paperback)

54 53 52 51   22 23 24

Printed in China   62
First edition, January 2008
Edited by Sheila Keenan
Book design by Kazu Kibuishi and Phil Falco
Creative Director: David Saylor

PROLOGUE

WHUD!

7

8

BOOK ONE
THE STONEKEEPER

2 YEARS LATER

18

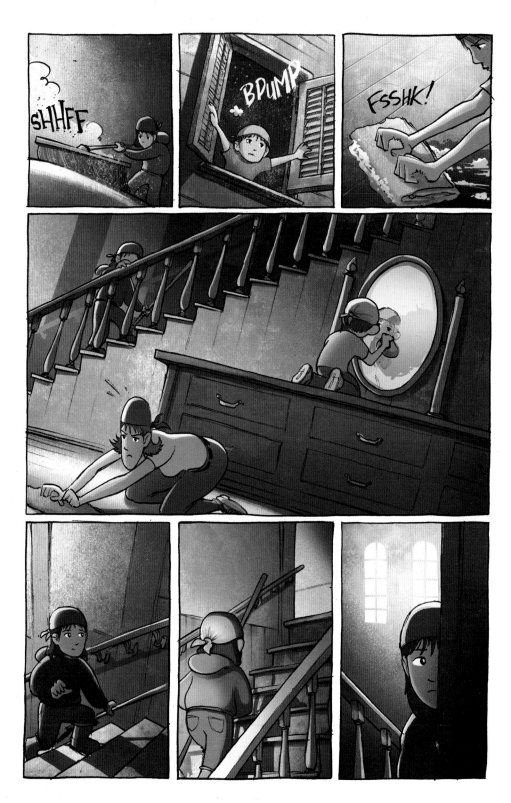

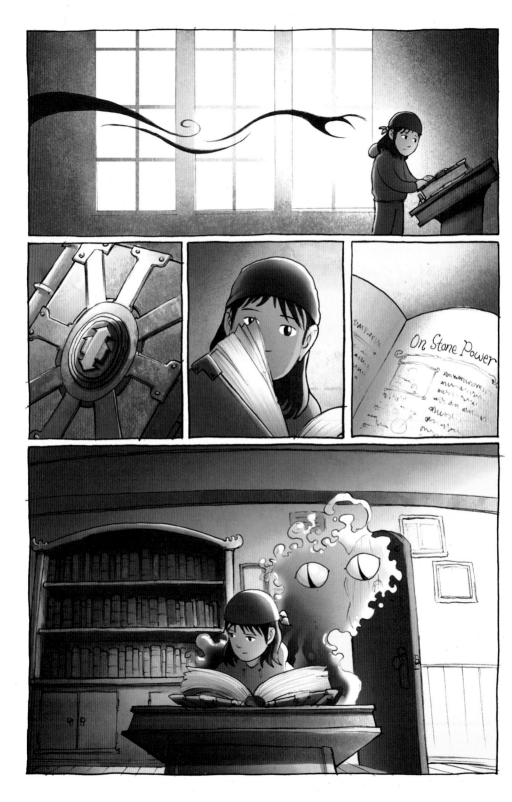

On Stone Power

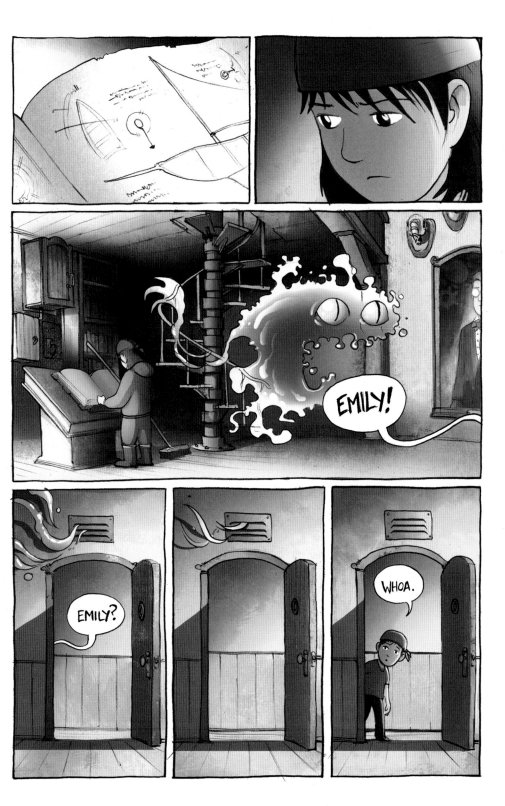

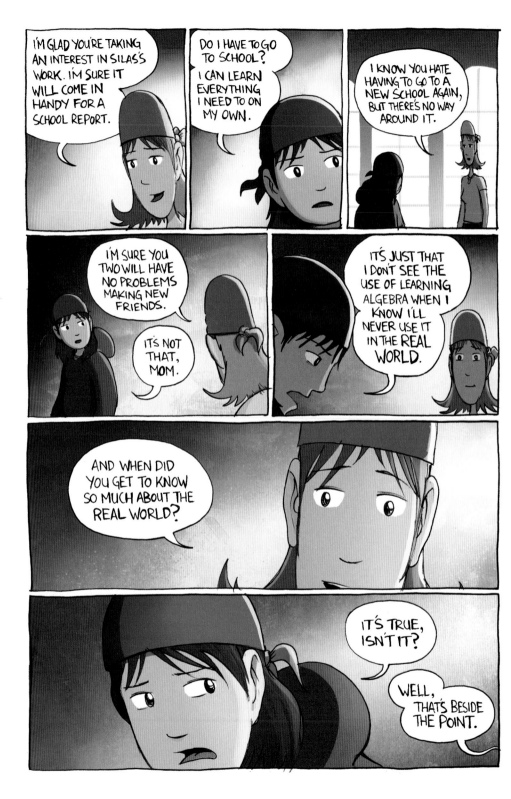

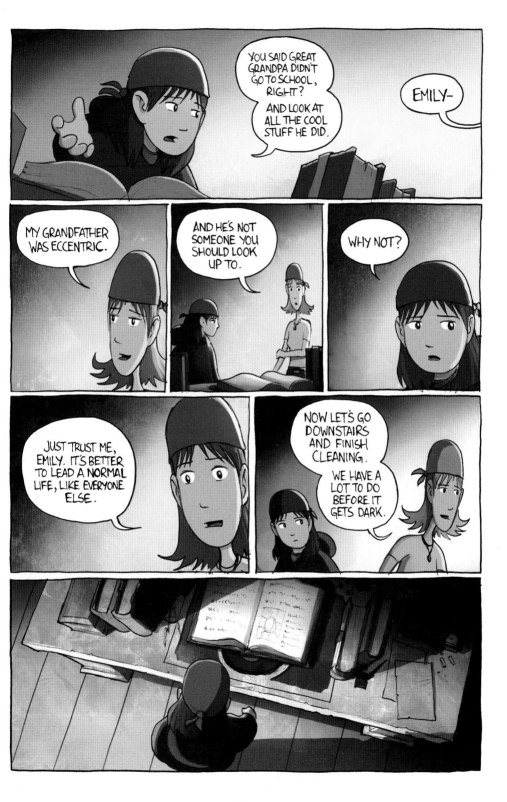

34

36

37

39

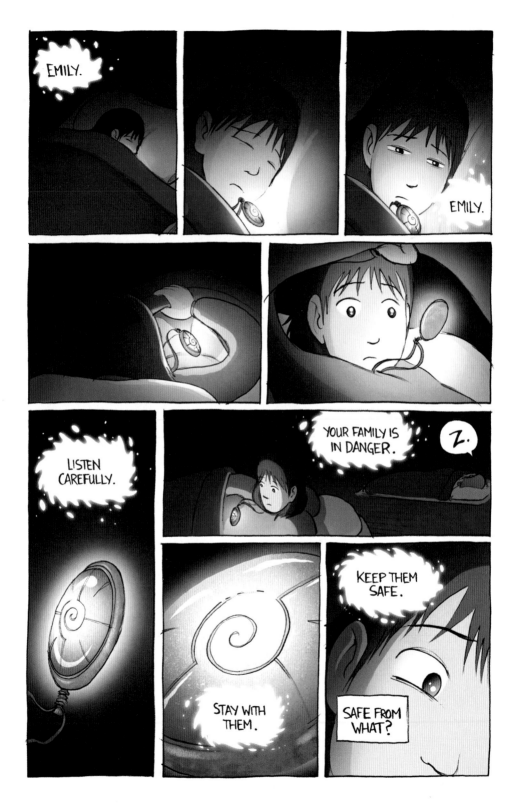

42

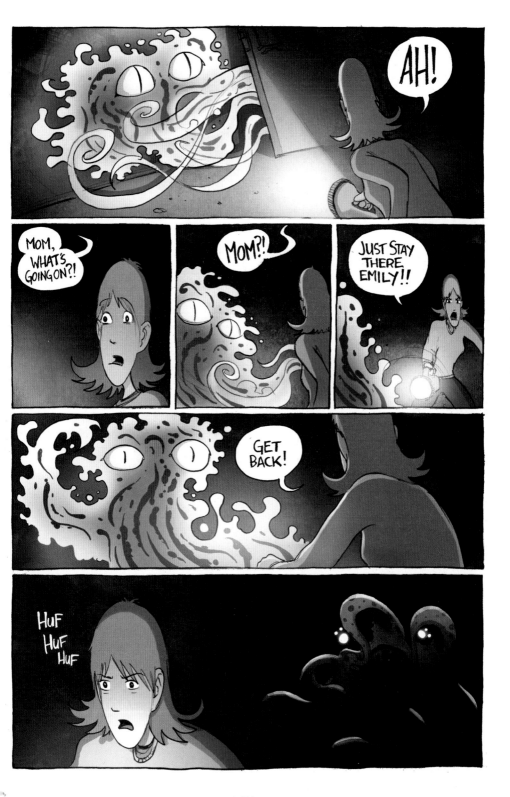

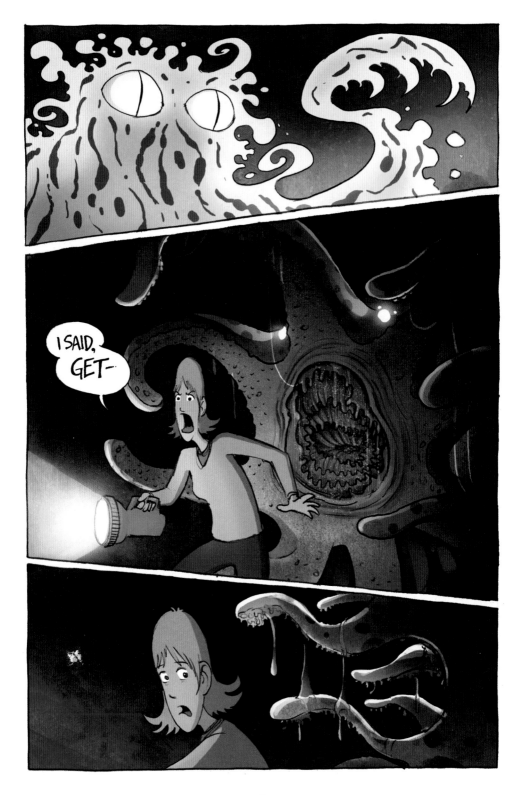

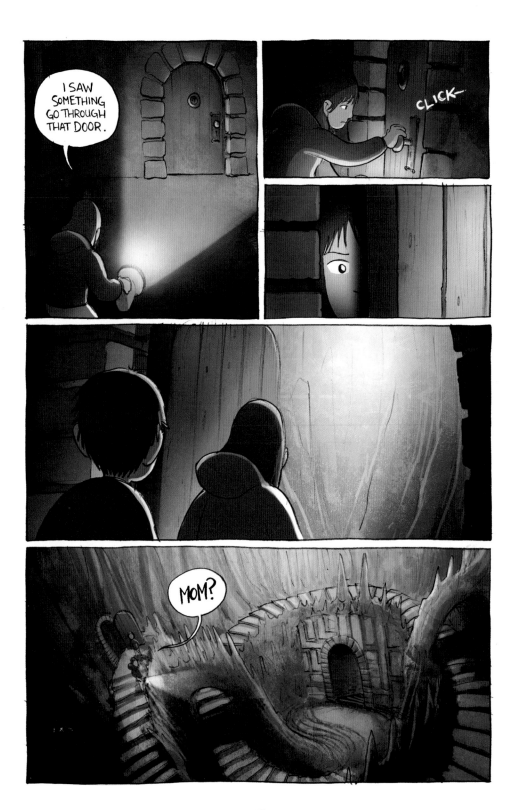

48

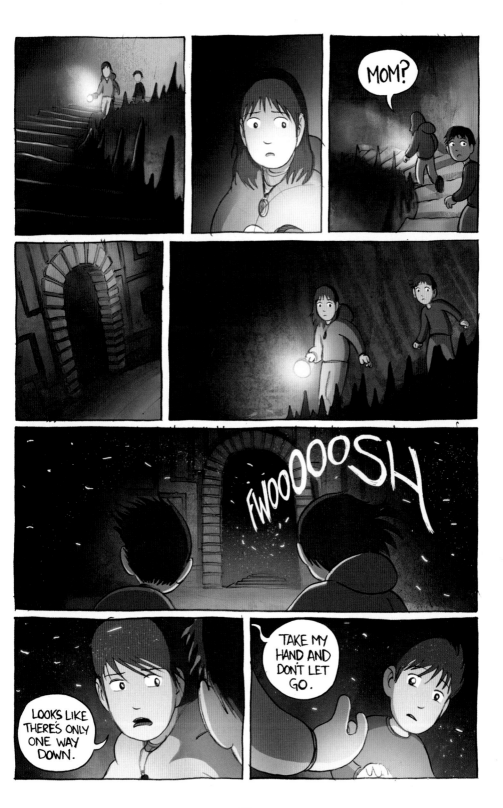

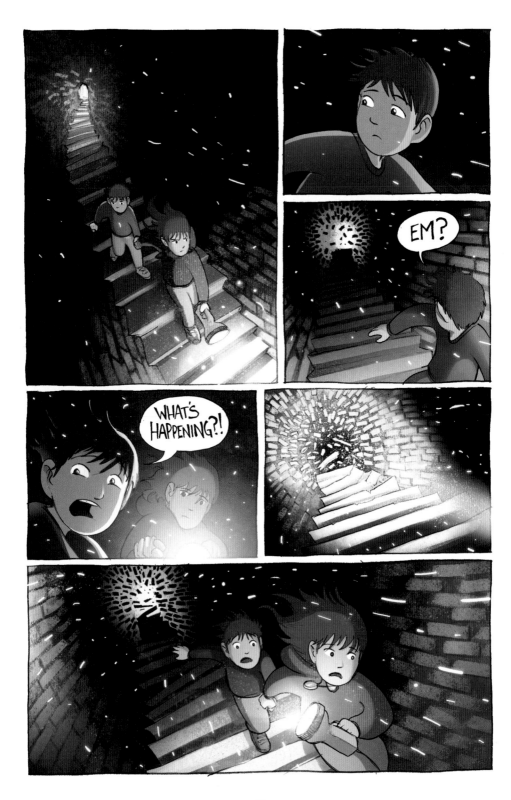

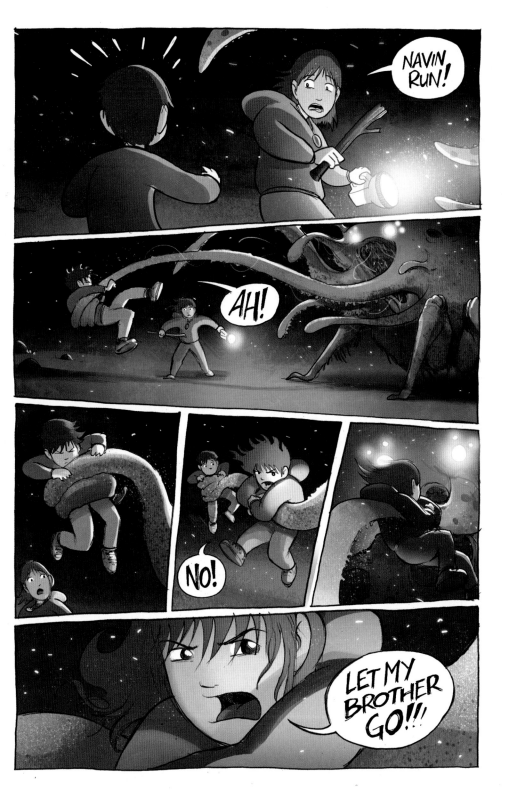

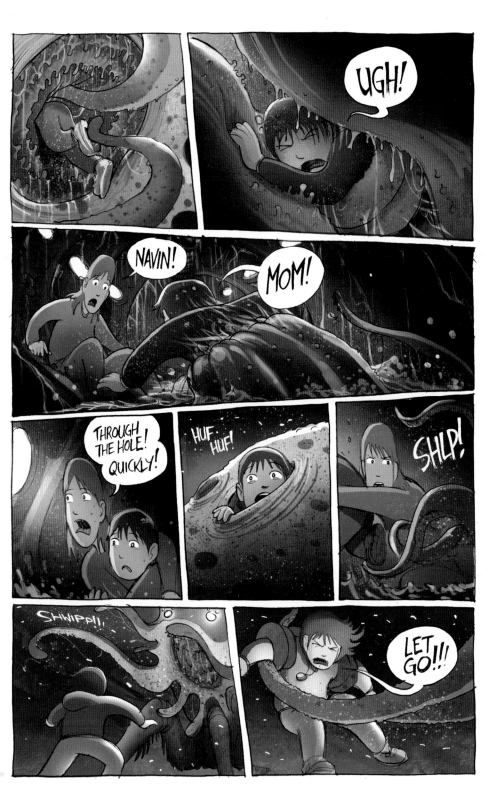

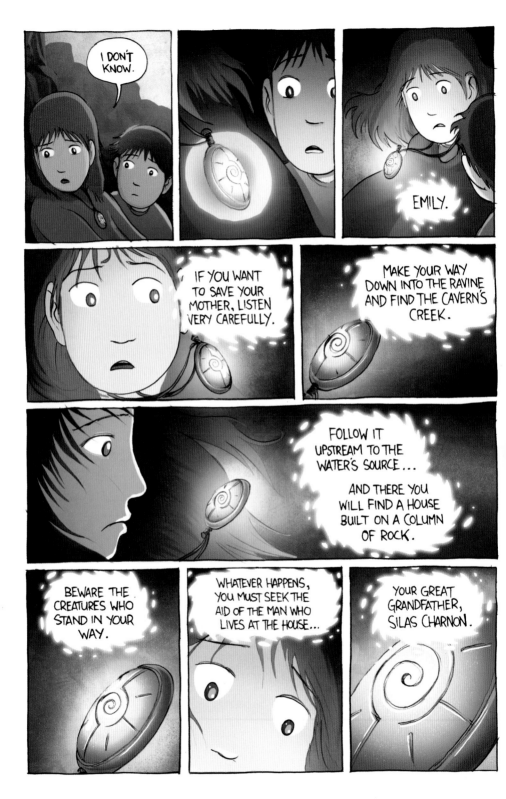

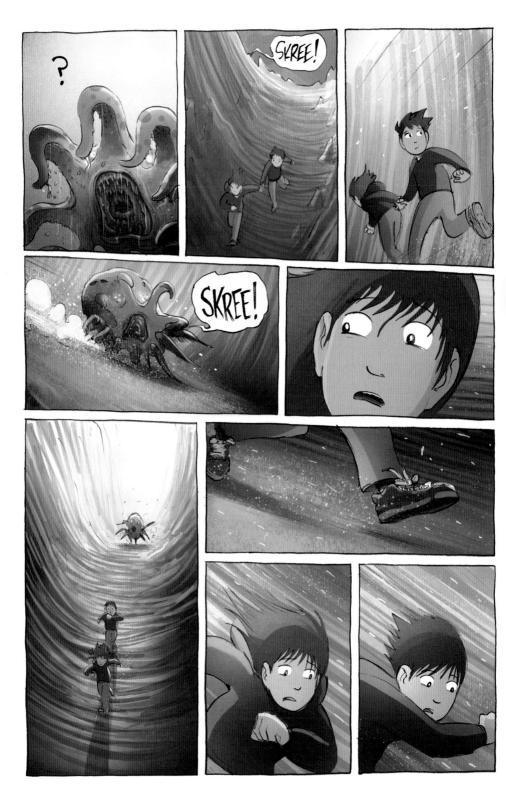

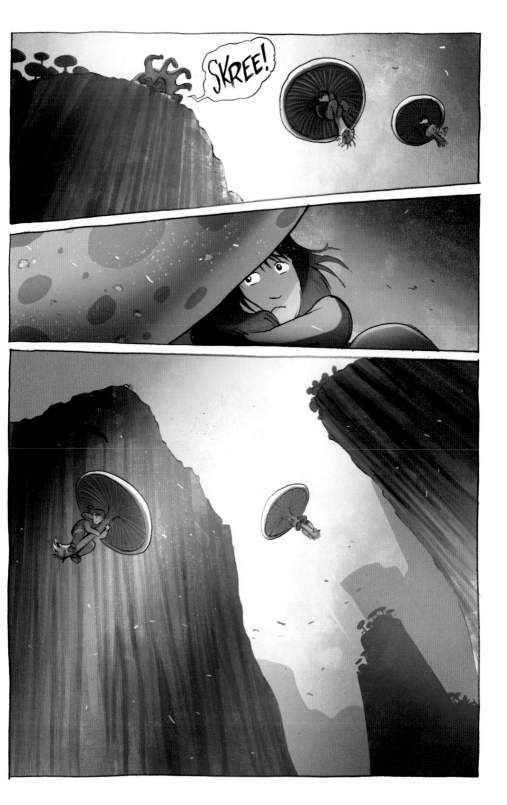

CHOMP!

FSSSHHHHH

FSHHHH.

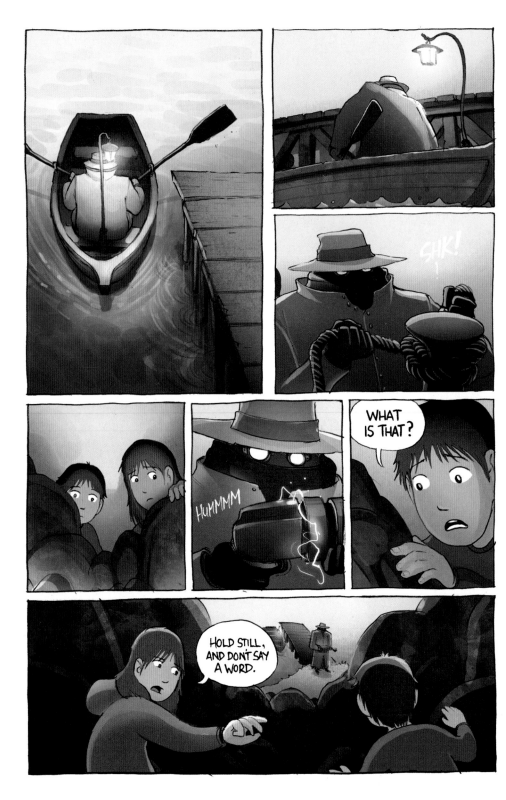

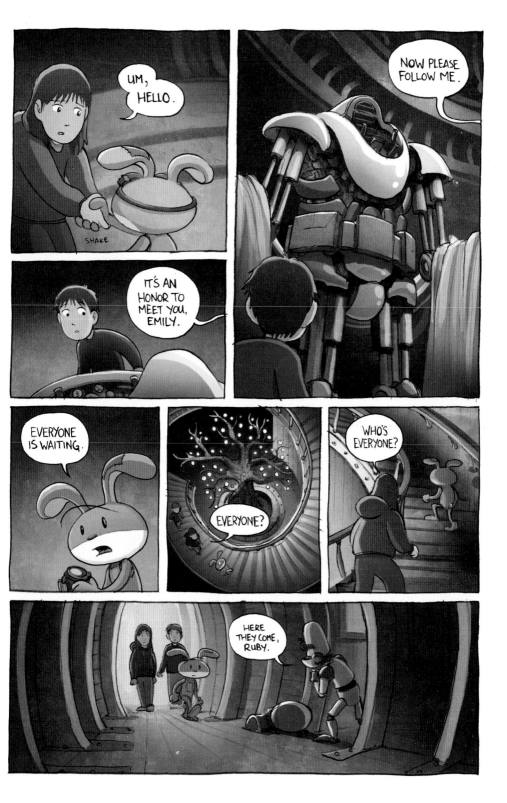

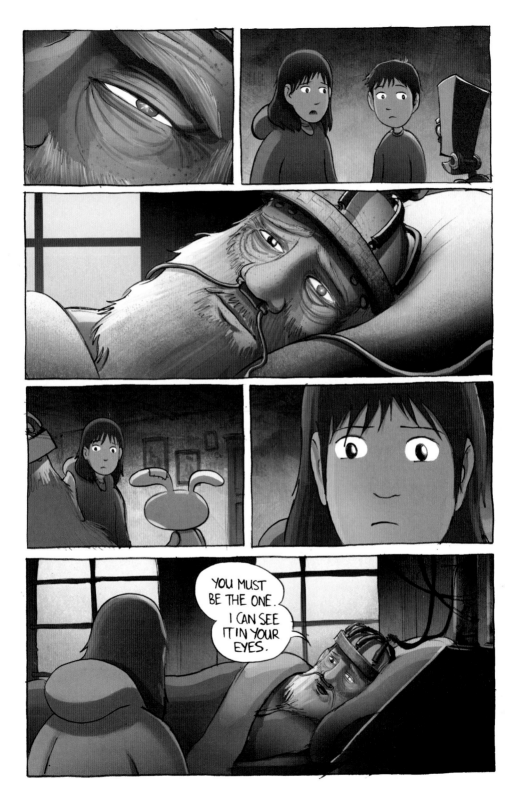

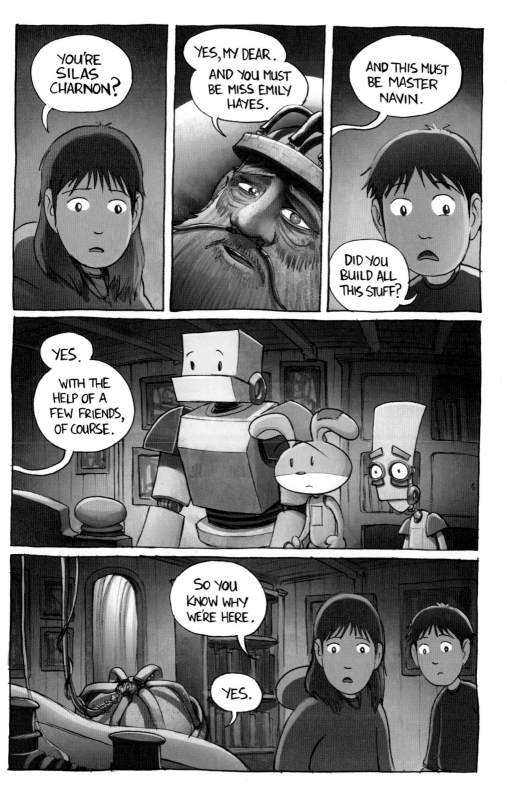

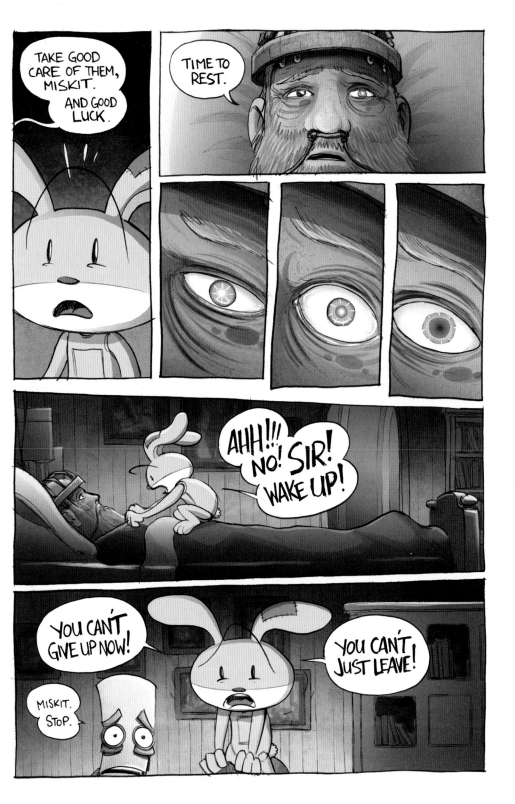

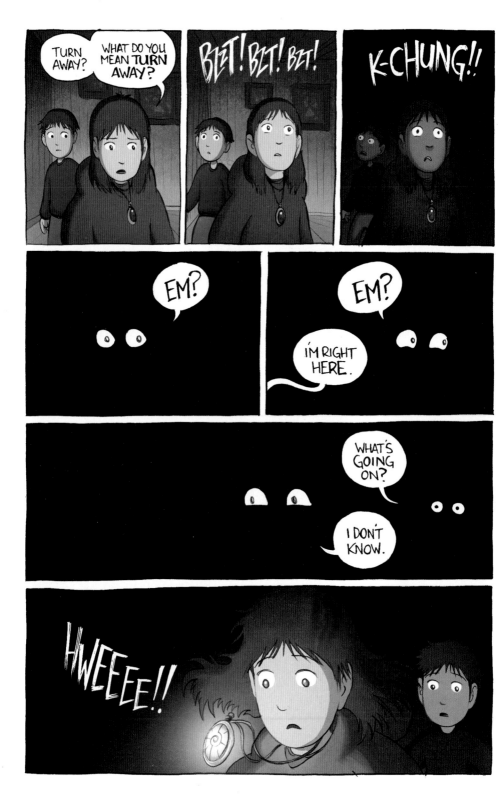

SZT!

SZT!

SZT!

WELCOME
ABOARD,
YOUNG
MASTER.

HWEEE...

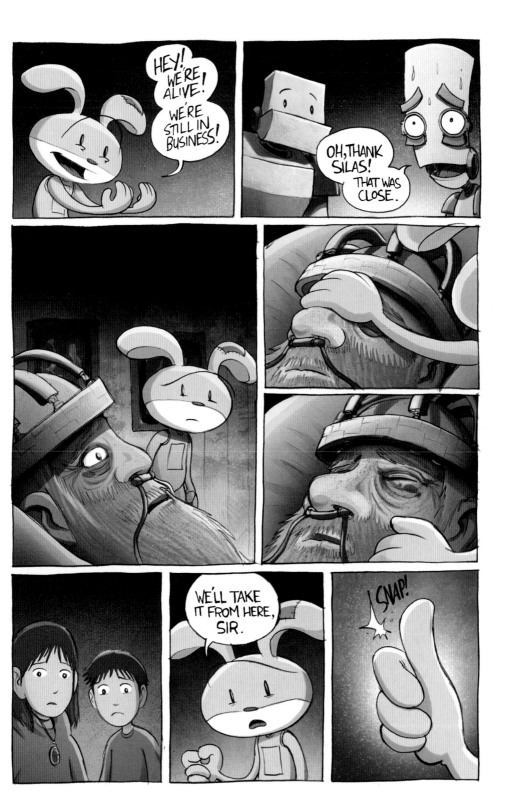

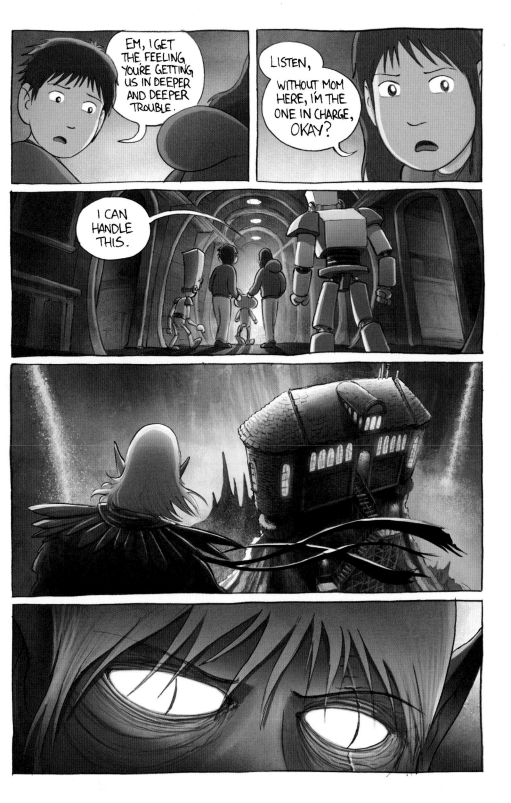

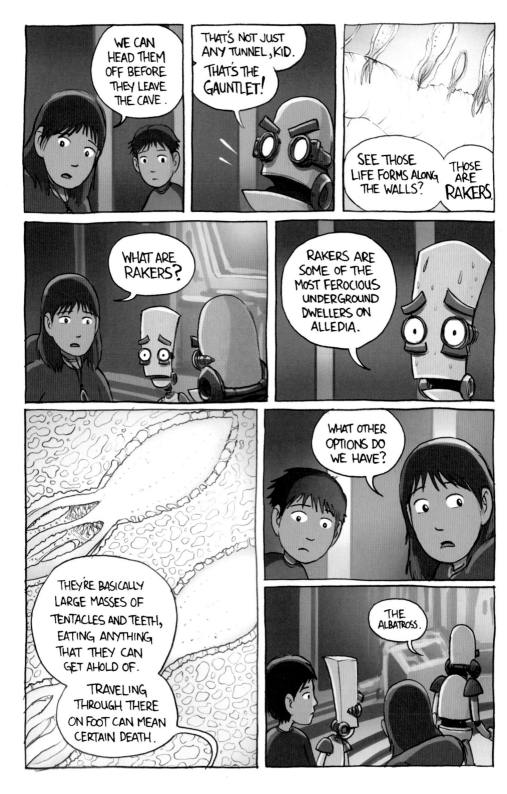

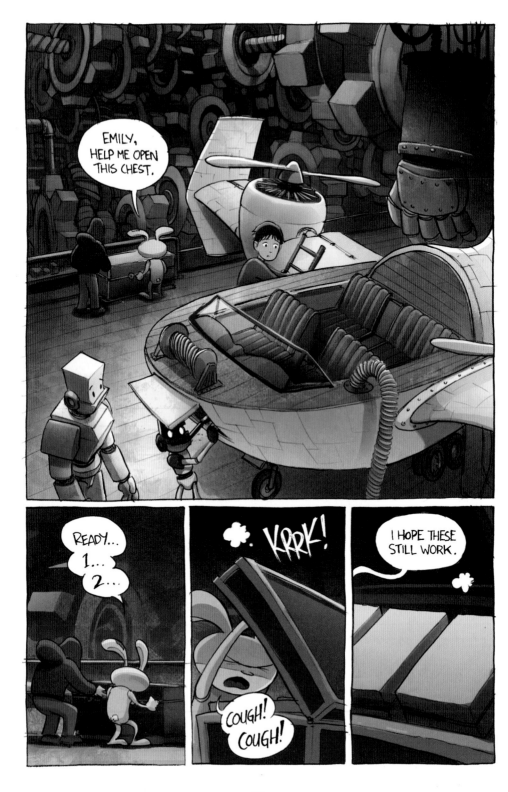

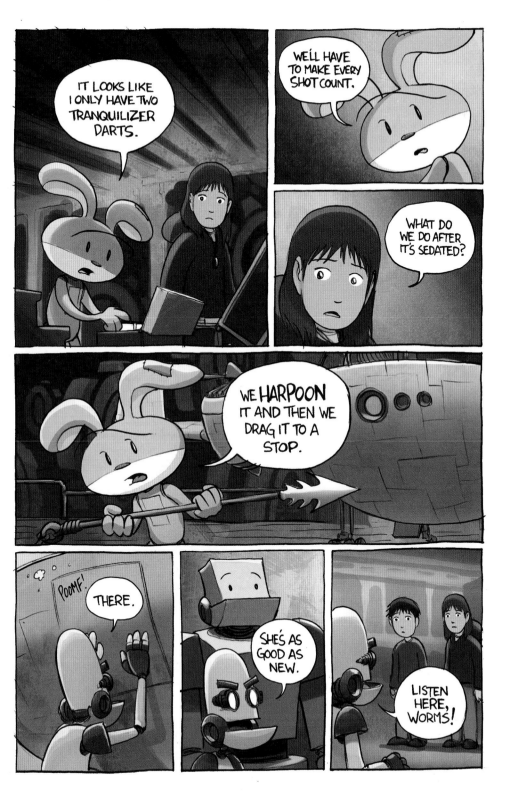

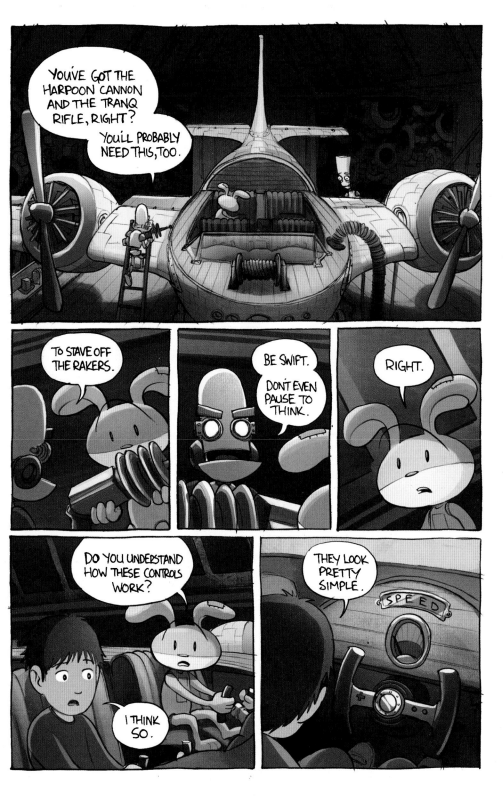

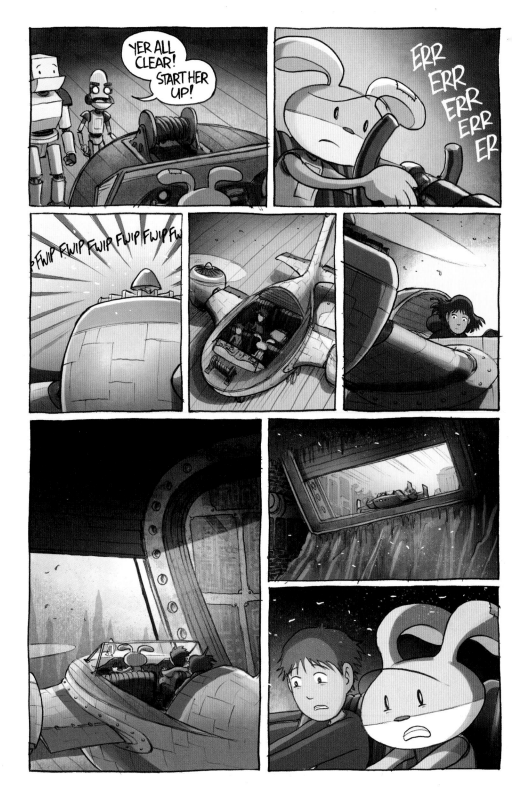

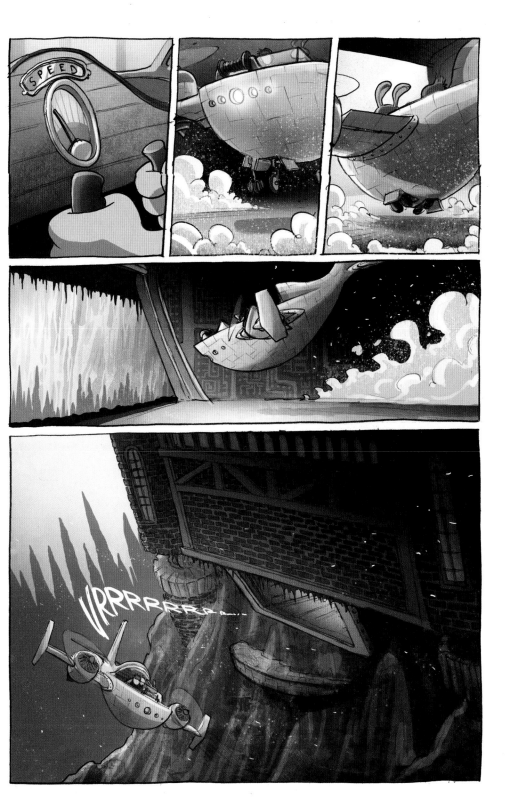

SPAK!!

GOTCHA!

ARE YOU
ALL RIGHT?

I THINK
SO, YES.

HEY
GUYS-

IT'S GETTING
CROWDED UP
HERE.

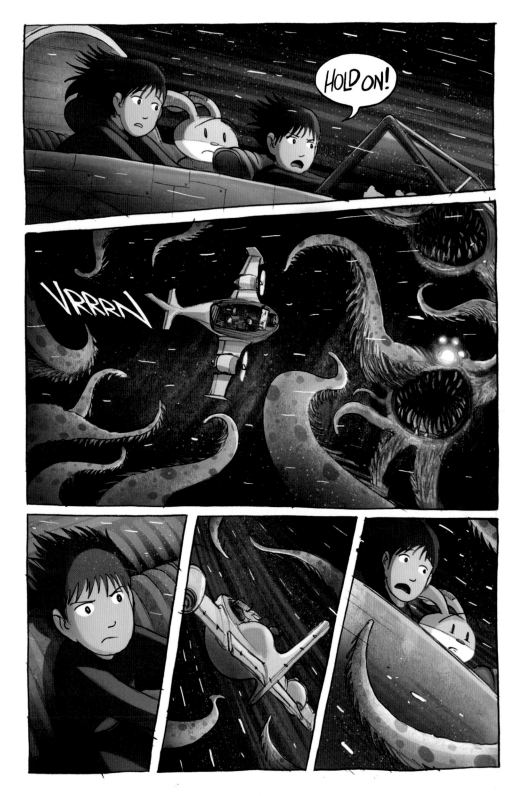

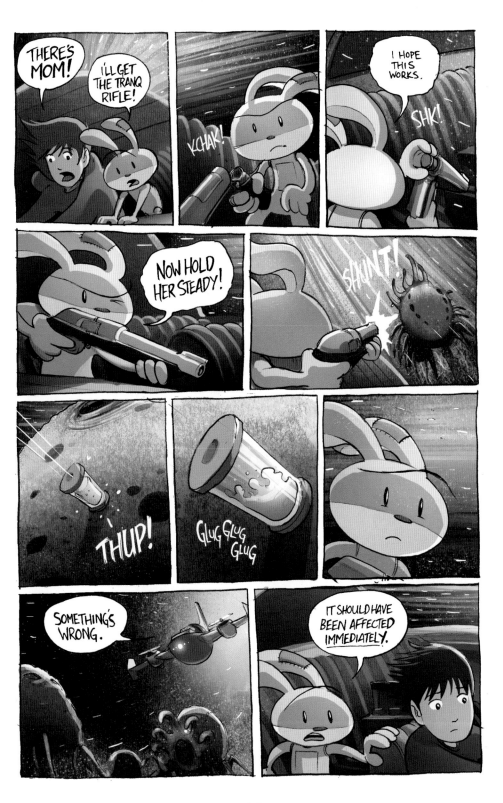

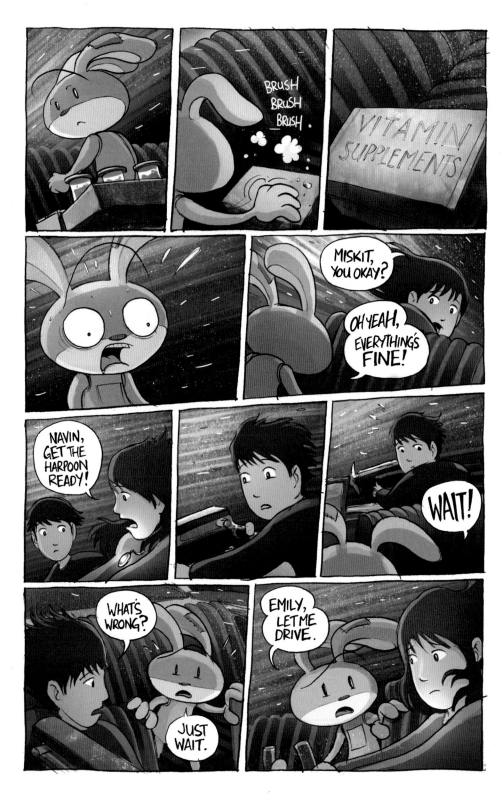

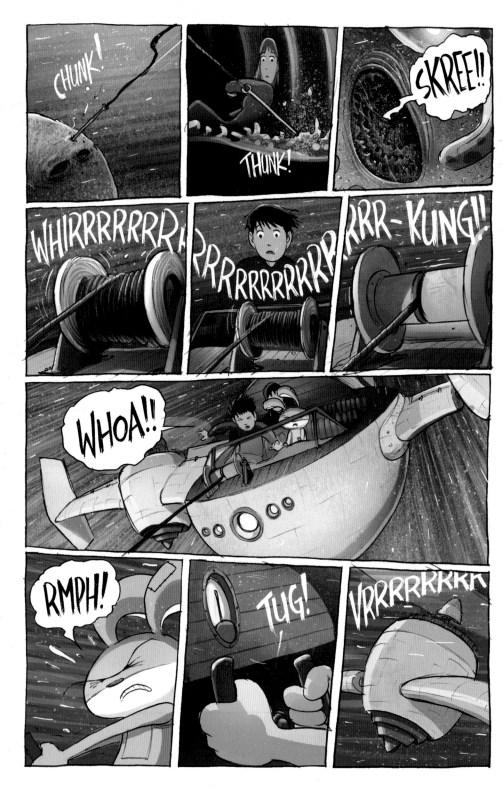

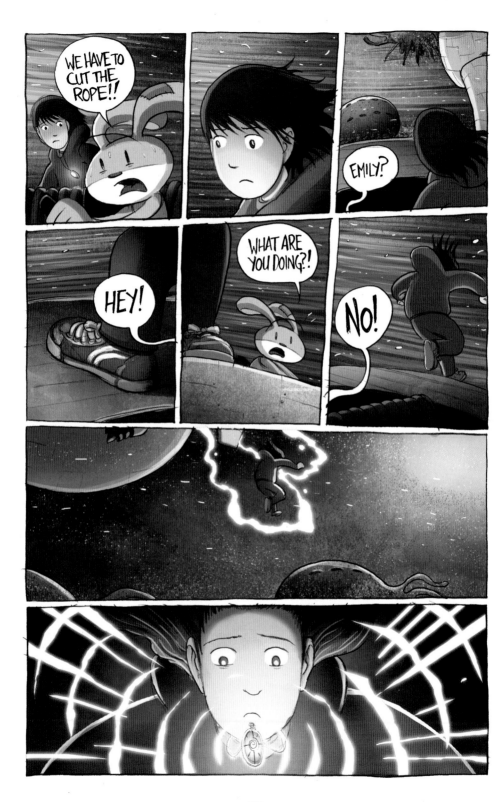

143

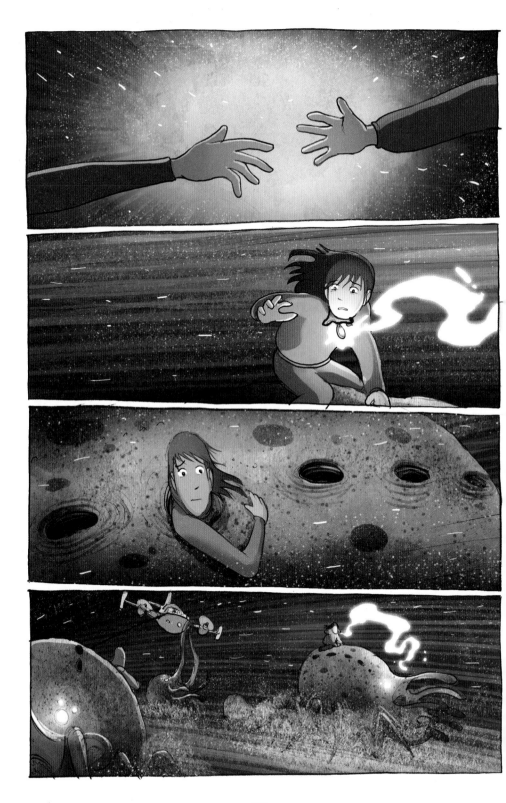

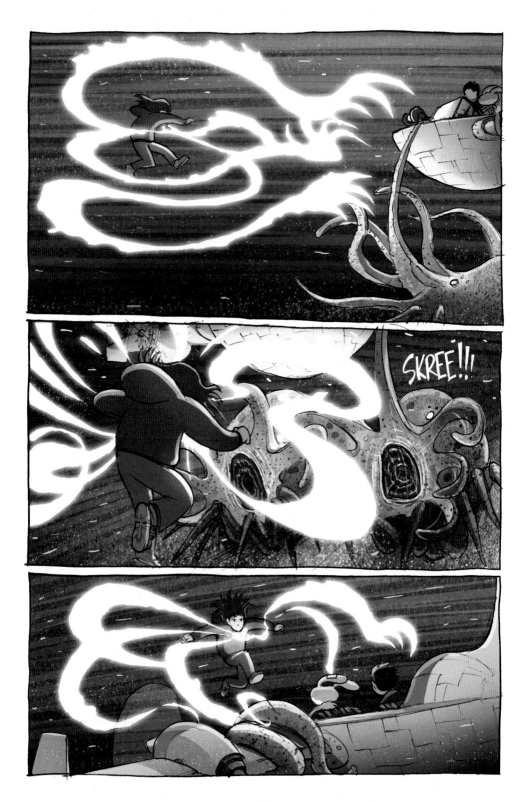

SKREE!!!

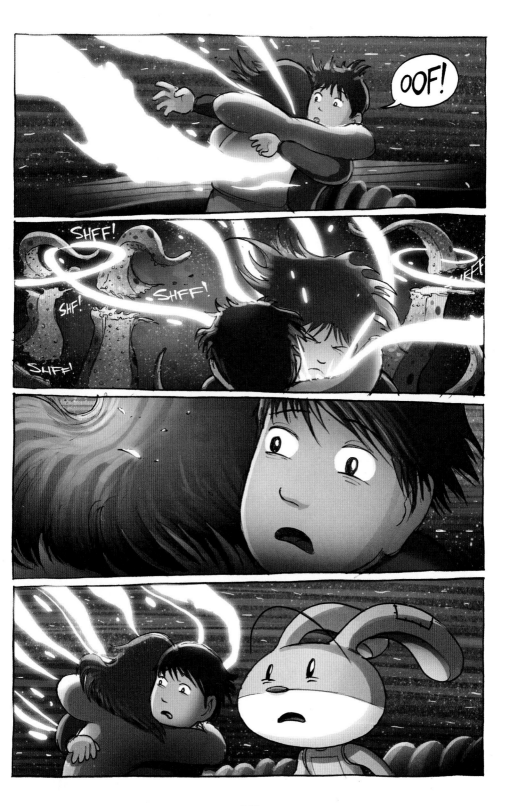

177

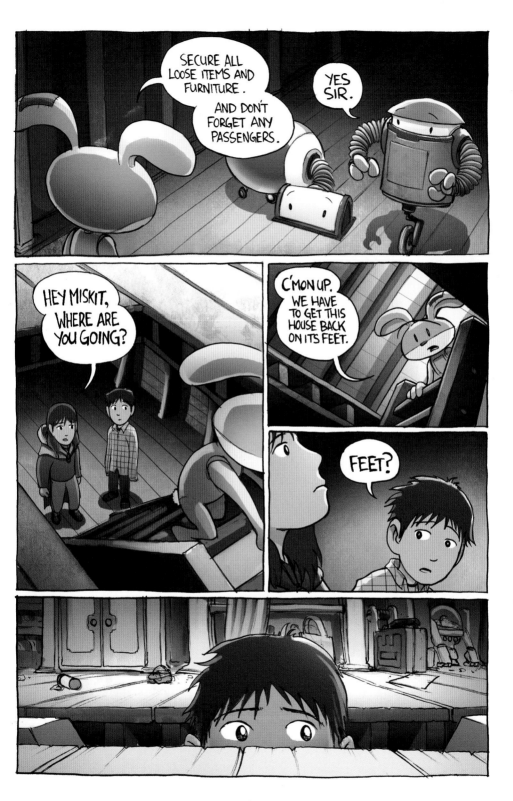

179

180

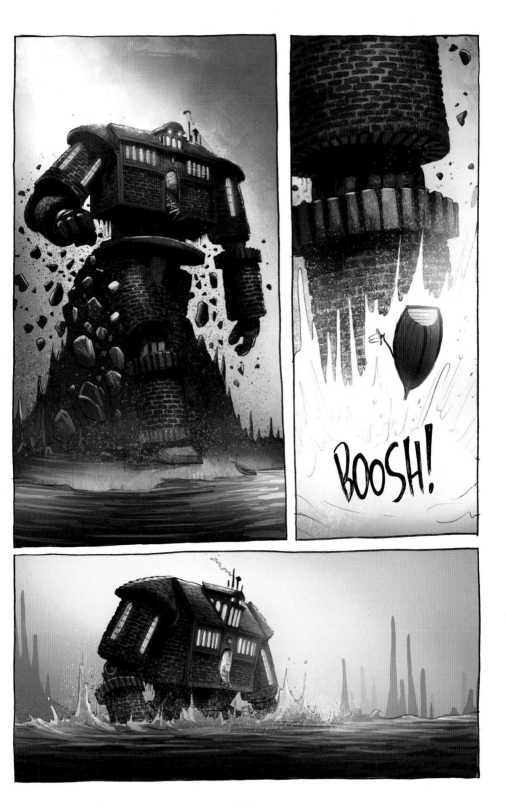

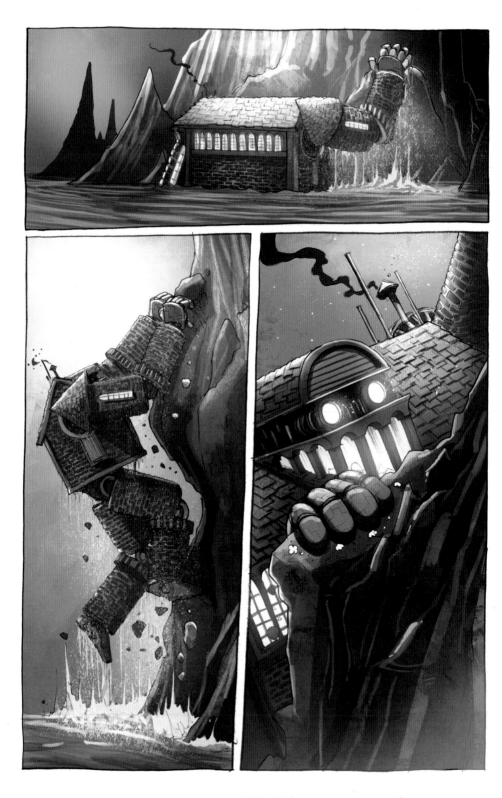

END OF BOOK ONE

ACKNOWLEDGMENTS

The production of this book was a team effort.

A very special thanks to Alan Beadle, Katy Wu, Arree Chung, Erik Martin, Dawn Fujioka, Dave Au, Sho Katayama, Kean Soo, Sarah Mensinga, Matthew Armstrong, Molly Hahn, Shadi Muklashy and Chris Appelhans for lending a hand in the completion of this book. Without these people, I would probably still be toiling away in a little room, trying to finish it. Most of all, I would like to thank my wife Amy, who painted the colors of many of the pages you hold in your hands, and who has been my biggest inspiration in creating this book.

More thanks go to Taka Kibuishi, Judy Hansen, Sheila Keenan, Janna Morishima, Scott McCloud, Jeff Smith, Ben Zhu, Phil Craven, and David Saylor for their support and patience. Thanks everyone!